The Soldier

THE KOREAN WAR SOLDIER AT HEARTBREAK RIDGE

By Carl R. Green and William R. Sanford

Illustrations by George Martin

Edited by Jean Eggenschwiler
and Kate Nelson

PUBLISHED BY

Capstone Press

Mankato, MN, U.S.A.

Distributed By
ℂℙ CHILDRENS PRESS®
CHICAGO

CIP

LIBRARY OF CONGRESS CATALOGING IN PUBLICATION DATA

Sanford, William R. (William Reynolds), 1927-
The Korean War soldier at Heartbreak Ridge / by William R.
Sanford, Carl R. Green.
p. cm.--(The Soldier)
Summary: Follows one soldier through the Korean War.
ISBN 1-56065-006-0
1. Korean War, 1950-1953--Juvenile literature. 2. Korean War,
1950-1953. 3. Soldiers. I. Green, Carl R. II. Title. III. Series:
Sanford, William R. (William Reynolds), 1927- Soldier.
DS918.S26 1989
951.904'2--dc20   89-25415 CIP AC

PHOTO CREDITS

Harry S. Truman Library: 10
U.S.Army Transportation Museum: 41

Illustrated by George Martin
Designed by Nathan Y. Jarvis & Associates, Inc.

Capstone Press

Box 669, Mankato, MN, U.S.A. 56001

CONTENTS

COMMUNISM THREATENS THE PEACE

When World War II ended, the world's people longed for a lasting peace. Two world wars in thirty years had caused too much death and suffering. The United States put its hopes for the future in the **United Nations**. If two countries fell into a dispute, the U.N. would help settle the argument.

The U.S. ran true to form after the war. "Bring the boys home!" the public said. The nation's citizen-soldiers turned in their uniforms. They went back to their families, found jobs, or entered college. The nation's economy boomed. Factories worked around the clock to fill the demand for cars, clothes, and cribs.

The hard-won peace did not last long. Headlines soon told of new troubles in the world. The Soviet Union took control of Eastern Europe. Poland and Hungary were among the countries that became communist puppets. In Asia, communists gained control of China. Was communism about to take over the rest of the world? The threat seemed very real.

Many Americans were alarmed. President Harry Truman gave money and guns to countries that resisted communism. This policy brought the U.S. into conflict with the Soviet Union and China. Newspapers called this non-shooting struggle the Cold War.

Franklin "Ben" Moore was not worried about the Cold War. He was thinking of his own future. Born in 1932, he grew up during the hard times of the Great Depression. Now it was 1950 and he was about to finish high school. It was time to think about finding a good job. Emmet Moore, his father, worked in the Senate Office Building as a janitor. He often told his son that he could grow up to be a senator some day. Ben just shook his head. Who ever heard of a black man being elected to Congress?

All his life Ben had gone to school in

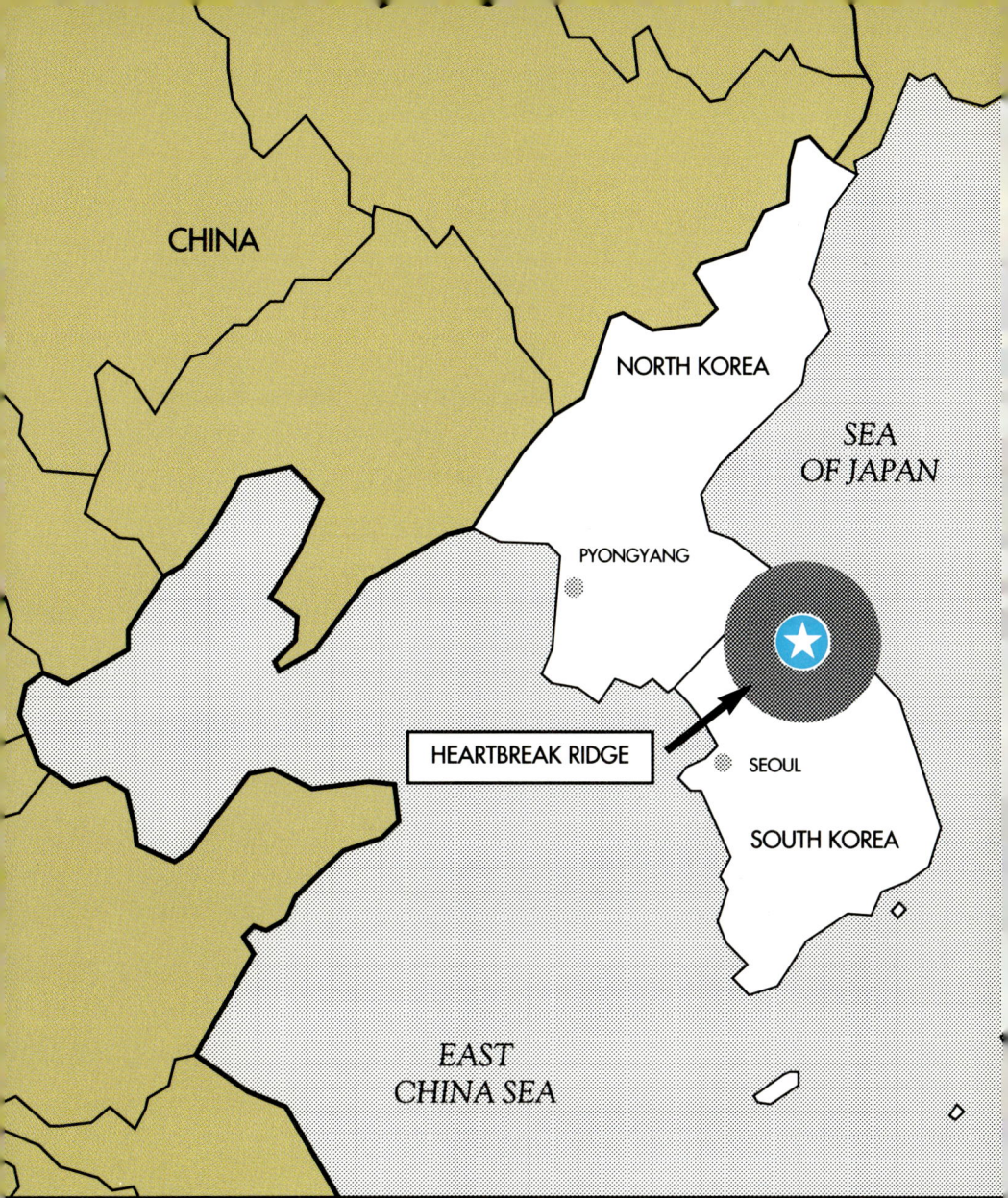

South Korea, Heartbreak Ridge and the surrounding
battle area.

Virginia. His classes were always divided by race. A few teachers had been white, but he had never had a white classmate. A math teacher told him he had a good head for numbers.

"You can be an engineer," Mrs. Simms had said. But college was an impossible dream, Ben knew. Where would his family find the money to pay for it? "Maybe I'll join the army and learn a skill," Ben told himself. "Uncle Sam can teach me to be a mechanic."

THE COLD WAR
TURNS HOT

After Ben graduated, Emmet took his family on a trip. They toured George Washington's home at Mount Vernon. Then they drove on to see some Civil War battlefields. Ben had not wanted to make the trip, but he began to enjoy himself. "Seeing these places makes history seem more real," he said to his mom.

On June 25 the Moores were packing to go home. Ben turned on the radio, hoping to find some music. He was just in time to catch a news flash.

"Today," the announcer said, "North Korean troops crossed the border into South Korea. Armed with Soviet-made weapons, they are driving toward Seoul. The South Korean capital may fall at any time. Now here's Dudley Pfeiffer in Washington."

The reporter reviewed the problem. "U.S. and Soviet troops moved into Korea at the end of World War II," he said. "We set up a free government in South Korea. The Russians turned North Korea into a communist state. They refused to allow free

President Harry S. Truman and General Douglas MacArthur.

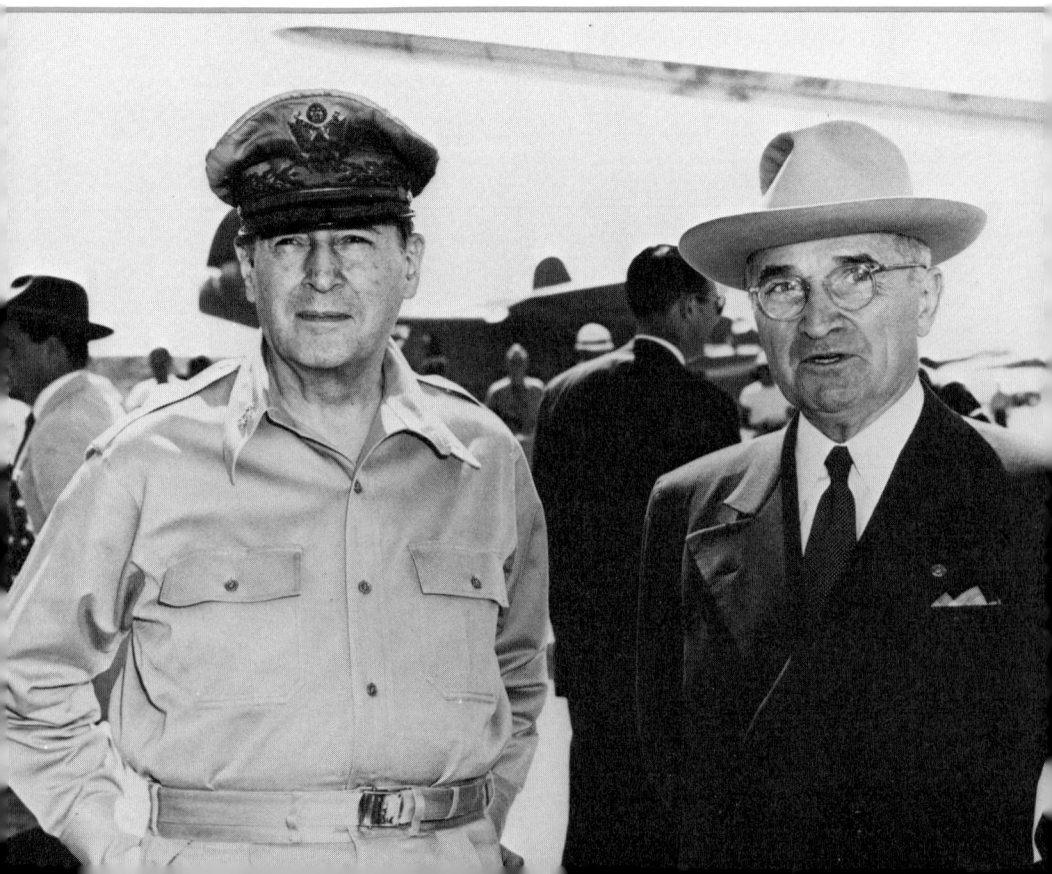

elections. As a result, the country is still divided."

"In 1946 the U.S. said it would stay in Korea until the nation was reunited," Pfeiffer went on. "But President Truman withdrew our forces a year ago. What will he do now to resist this new communist aggression?"

"Let the Koreans fight it out," Emmett said. He snapped off the radio. "We don't want to fight another foreign war."

Many Americans shared Emmett's feelings. President Truman had other ideas. He said the U.S. could not let the communists take whatever they wanted. He ordered General Douglas MacArthur to send naval and air units to help South Korea. In the U.N. the Security Council said the invasion was a threat to world peace. The council voted to ask its members to defend South Korea.

A week later, Ben and Herbie Jackson were coming home from a baseball game. "Hey," Herbie said, "old man Smith has a TV turned on in his store window. Come on, let's take a look."

Televisions were rare in this part of town. Ben and Herbie stood on the sidewalk and watched a small black-and-white set.

"Looks like more war news," Herbie complained. "Why doesn't Smith turn on a comedy show?"

The announcer pointed to a map of Korea. "Seoul fell on the fourth day of the war," he said. "The President ordered American ground forces into Korea on June 30. The call went to the 8th Army in Japan, which experts say is poorly prepared for battle. Ready or not, the U.S. 24th Infantry reached Korea yesterday. The troops landed at the southern port of Pusan [poo-san]."

The map showed how quickly the North Koreans were pushing southward. "We've got to stop them," Ben said.

As if he had heard the comment, the announcer changed the subject. "In Washington," he said, "Congress extended the draft law. The goal is to build the nation's armed forces to over three million. The President was also given the power to call army reserve units to active duty."

Ben snapped his fingers. "That does it," he said. "I'm joining up."

"Not this child," Herbie said. "Uncle Sam will have to come and get me. And I'll be hard to find."

"If he wants you, he'll get you," Ben

laughed. "You're registered for the **draft**, same as me. Now that we're 19, they're sure to call us up for two years of active duty."

Herbie pointed to a Cadillac parked by the curb. "The draft wouldn't get me if I was rich," he said. "I could go to college and get a **deferment**. It's the young, poor guys who can't beat the system. I'm not putting my life on the line to save South Korea."

"Hey, someone has to stop the Commies!" Ben said. "If it wasn't South Korea, it might be closer to home. I'll go to the recruiting office in the morning."

Everything happened fast. In early July Ben raised his right hand and was sworn into the U.S. Army. An hour later he was on a bus to Fort Dix, New Jersey.

The first day went by in a blur. Ben saw three men faint when the doctors gave them their shots. A barber shaved Ben's head. A supply sergeant loaded him down with clothing and bedding. At his **barracks** he was given a bunk and a locker.

The recruits jogged wherever they went. The army called it "double-timing." Ben did not mind. The fresh air and exercise made him think of summer camp. The starchy meals and hard work added pounds to his slender 6'4" frame. At times he dozed during lectures, but he enjoyed the drills and the rifle range. At night he played basketball with men from a dozen different states.

It was not all fun and games. Pulling KP (kitchen police) meant long days of washing greasy dishes. On Friday nights the company held "**GI** parties." These "parties" meant hours of scrubbing, cleaning, and polishing. A slip-up during inspection brought extra duties. After a sloppy shave cost him a day of KP, Ben was more careful.

The young soldier's test scores caught a captain's eye. The captain gave Ben a chance to go to clerk-typist school. Ben turned him down. He said he wanted to be a foot soldier.

"With a war on, the infantry is a cinch to see combat," the captain reminded him.

"Yes, sir!" Ben said. "I joined the army to fight."

At the end of basic training, Ben got his wish. His company was ordered to report to Fort Lewis, Washington. There they would board a ship bound for Japan. Korea was the next stop after that.

PREPARING FOR COMBAT

Before reporting to Fort Lewis, Ben went home on leave. The war news worried his mother.

"The Americans and South Koreans have pulled back to Pusan," she said. "All their supplies have to be unloaded there. It's the only port still open."

"Stop worrying, Mom," Ben said. "Our lines are holding. We'll soon send those North Koreans back where they came from."

Ben's dad had a second worry. "This is the first time whites and blacks have served side by side," he said. "Has anyone given you a bad time?"

"There are a few loudmouths in any unit," Ben said with a shrug. "Some of the guys call me 'Big Ben' because of my height. I

15

don't mind. There's one thing about the army. If you do your job, no one bothers you."

Soon after reaching Fort Lewis, Ben's company boarded a troop ship. The fun of taking a sea voyage faded when the ship hit rough water. Wedged into a bunk in a crowded compartment, Ben's stomach turned inside out. Before long, over half of the troops were just as sick as he was.

By the fifth day out Ben felt well enough to enjoy the sea air. He watched the waves and relaxed in the sun. Then the harsh voice of Sergeant Aaron cut into his daydreams. Aaron needed some men to mop the decks. Ben thought about "bugging out" of the work detail. If he did, and Aaron caught him, he would be put on report. Ben did not want to lose his promotion to Private First Class. He grabbed a mop and went to work.

Five days later the troops landed in Japan. Trucks took them to Camp Drake. In the barracks the men listened to soldiers who had fought in Korea. "Winter's coming," a corporal told them. "It's going to be like an icebox over there. To make it worse, Korea is mostly mountains and dirt roads."

"What about the **gooks**?" someone asked.

"Call the North Koreans 'gooks' if you want," the corporal said, "but they're good soldiers. They have first-rate equipment and they know how to use it."

The men were given advanced training at Camp Drake. Ben took a liking to the antitank rocket launcher. Better known as the bazooka, it was light and easy to carry. To

fire it, he held the weapon on his shoulder and took aim. His partner shoved the 3.4-pound missiles into the rear of the tube. When Ben squeezed the trigger, the rocket blasted a target 1,200 feet away.

The mortar was a useful weapon for Korea's mountains. Ben thought the 88-mm mortar looked like a piece of drain pipe. One soldier sighted and fired while a second man dropped in the 10.6-pound shells. A good team could drop 18 rounds a minute on a target 2,000 yards away.

The foot soldier's basic weapon was the **M-1 rifle**. Ben sharpened his shooting eye during long hours on the rifle range. He also trained with the M-3 submachine gun, hand **grenades**, and the flamethrower. The machine gun fired a deadly 450 rounds per minute. The M-1 was slower, but much more accurate. The grenades were small, hand-thrown bombs that weighed only 1.3 pounds. They exploded 4.5 seconds after Ben released the safety lever. Tossing grenades was easy compared to using the flamethrower. Ben shuddered each time he used the weapon. The thought of being touched by that bright tongue of flame was terrifying.

The training never let up. Ben learned

that fact the hard way during a field exercise. He stood up to watch some B-29 bombers flying overhead. Sergeant Aaron put a shoulder into Ben's stomach and knocked him down. "If you goof up like that in combat, you're a dead man!" Aaron yelled.

Ben's **platoon** formed into an assault squad and a support squad. The support squad gave covering fire to the assault squad when it attacked the "enemy." Radio operators kept the squads in contact. Over and over the men ran through all phases of the attack. They even recovered men pretending to be wounded. It was an iron-clad rule: no man should ever be left behind.

Ben learned to dig a **foxhole** while under fire. It was easy to keep his head down with machine gun bullets whistling above him. Aaron taught him to throw the earth in a wide circle. "Piles of dirt will give away your position," the sergeant said.

On September 15, 1950 cheers echoed through the barracks. General MacArthur had landed an invasion force at Inchon, the port city of Seoul. Ben looked at a map and cheered along with his buddies. Inchon was 200 miles behind the North Korean front lines. The U.N. forces were striking back.

THE CHINESE ENTER
THE WAR

Ben worried that the war would be over before he got into the fighting. The Inchon landing had turned the tide. By early October the American and South Korean forces were driving northward.

His orders came late that month. He was one of 40 riflemen being sent to the 2nd Division. The men were nervous as they packed their duffle bags. The chances were good that they were replacing men who had been killed or wounded.

The replacements flew to Korea on a crowded transport plane. After landing near Seoul they climbed out and grabbed their gear. "Now where do we go?" Ben asked his buddy Mark Lawson.

"Beats me," Mark said. "Maybe that guard knows." The Korean guard turned to face the two black men. He had a strong, square face and was barely five feet tall. His breath told them he had been eating *kimchi*. Ben had read about the Korean national dish of pickled cabbage. As Sergeant Aaron had warned them, it was smelly.

"Where are the trucks for 2nd Division?"

The guard's blank look told them he did not understand. Ben asked his question again, speaking more slowly. "Okay, GI, 2nd Division number one!" the Korean said with a smile. He pointed to a line of trucks behind a hangar.

Ben and Mark hauled their gear to the trucks. The driver said they were joining the 2nd on its way to the Yalu River.

"Isn't Red China on the far side of the Yalu?" Mark asked.

"Don't worry about the Chinese," the driver said. "This war will be over by Christmas."

Ben, Mark, and the other men joined the division north of Pyongyang [pea-AWNG-yang]. Along the way, they saw a land of mountains, villages, and rice paddies. Ben met his new platoon and fell into its routines. Their patrols met only light North Korean resistance. When he was shot at Ben found that he kept his nerve. Some men froze when they came under fire. Ben gritted his teeth and kept moving.

On Thanksgiving Day, the field kitchens served hot turkey dinners. After days of eating canned **C-rations**, the meal was a treat. "It's not like my mom's turkey," Ben joked. "That's okay. I'm still going back for seconds."

While they ate, the men talked about the latest rumors. "I hear the Chinese might come south to help the North Koreans," Mark said. "What if they throw a million troops at us? No one knows the real size of their People's Liberation Army."

Corporal Andy Dawes peeled an orange and shook his head. "Nah," he drawled, "the PLA generals are smart. They know we'll use atomic bombs if they come south. I bet President Truman and General MacArthur have it all planned. Truman dropped A-bombs on Japan to end World War II. If China attacks, he'll do it again."

"It's different now," Ben argued. "Back in 1945, only the U.S. had the bomb. Now the Soviet Union has it, too. What if they back up the Chinese and start an atomic war?"

"It won't come to that," Andy insisted. "The North Koreans are beaten. If the Chinese come in, we'll whip them, too."

He was wrong on both counts. In late November, Chinese troops slipped into North Korea. Two days after Thanksgiving they struck all along the front. The massive assault sent the U.N. forces reeling backward. As Ben had guessed, Truman did not order the use of atomic weapons.

The new men saw their first real action. The 2nd Division was covering the retreat. Ben was soon cursing the cold, the rocky hills, and the bugle-blowing Chinese. The unit lost many men and most of its big guns on the way south.

The retreat was a nightmare. Ben learned to sleep in trucks that jolted over bumpy roads. By mid-December the U.N. forces were back near the 38th parallel. On New Year's Day half a million Chinese and North Korean troops launched a new attack. Seoul and Inchon fell for the second time.

In late January of 1951 the U.N. forces steadied and held. Soon they returned to the attack. Seoul was recaptured in March. Then the drive stalled and the two armies dug in. The front lay along a line 20 miles north of the 38th parallel.

On May 15 Ben and his buddies were almost overrun by a **"human sea" attack**. Masses of Chinese came at them like a spring flood. The Americans, with help from Dutch and Belgian troops, held their positions. For three days the Chinese charged into point-blank machine gun fire.

After that battle the 2nd was pulled off the line. Ben and Mark were told to pack their bags. They were among the men due for a Rest and Recuperation leave in Japan.

AN ARMY OF MANY NATIONS

Seven days of **R&R**! Ben and Mark checked into an army hotel in Tokyo. On the first morning they ate a breakfast of ham and eggs. After weeks at the front, fresh eggs were a luxury.

Dressed in their best uniforms, they went out to see the city. "Let's start with the Imperial Palace," Ben said. They caught a cab and quickly wished they had not. The cab driver drove his tiny car through heavy traffic at a breakneck speed.

Unlike the White House in Washington, D.C., the palace was closed to visitors. Ben took pictures of Mark posing by the moat.

Both of them were hungry, so they headed for a nearby restaurant. A hostess

dressed in a red kimono asked them to take
off their boots. In stocking feet they stepped
into a small room covered with straw tatami
mats. The only furniture was a low table. A
second woman showed them how to sit cross-
legged on a pillow.

Ben looked for a knife and fork but saw only wooden chopsticks. The woman, whose name was Yuki, showed them how to sip their soup from the bowl. Then she cooked a dish of thinly sliced beef and vegetables on a gas burner. "This is sukiyaki," she said. Ben found that the food was tasty and that chopsticks were easy to use. Mark had more trouble. His rice kept falling off into his lap. Yuki put her hand over her mouth when she laughed at his clumsiness.

The day was a great success. They shopped in a huge department store and visited a shrine. For dinner they tried raw fish. In the evening they danced at the hotel to a lively jazz band. The Japanese hostesses were young and pretty. No one seemed to care that Ben and Mark were black.

They were tired and happy when they got back to their room. "You know, this really is a United Nations army," Ben said. "Tonight I met soldiers from Turkey, Australia, and Greece. And I saw uniform patches from Colombia, France, and Great Britain. If we get shot, we might get fixed up by those medics from Sweden."

"Yeah, I was talking to a cook who works at the Reception Center," Mark laughed. "He has a tough job. The Turks can't eat pork, and the Indians won't eat beef. The French want their own bread, and the Filipinos want more rice. What's more, they ask for their food in over a dozen languages!"

R&R passed all too quickly. It was a shock to return to Korea and to army discipline. To Ben's relief, the 2nd was holding a quiet sector. That made life easier.

Ben walked to a Korean village one day with candy and cigarettes in his pack. He handed out the candy bars to a flock of ragged children. Then a boy led him to an old man who was selling carved jade. Six packs of cigarettes bought a pair of jade earrings.

"Kim Song thanks you," the man said with a bow.

Ben welcomed the chance to talk to a Korean. The man's English was a little strange, but Ben could understand it. "Your army fights very well," he said. "Why were the North Koreans able to push you back to Pusan in 1950?"

"Korea is very old country," Kim said. "Once we were free, but Japan rules us for many years. After Japan defeated us in 1945, we divided in two. Republic of Korea depends on Americans, but GI's go home. North Koreans have much more soldiers, five to one on front lines. They advance behind Russian-made tanks. We fight bravely, but small ROK army can only slow them down."

"Things are different now," Ben said.

"Yes," Kim agreed proudly. "Now we have twelve fine divisions. GI's come back and United Nations fight on our side. We will not stop until we have driven out the Chinese. Then we make Korea one free country."

FIGHT-FIGHT, TALK-TALK

"Fall in!" a sergeant bellowed. "Captain Fraser has something to say."

The men gathered on a windy hillside. They grumbled that they did not need one more lecture on avoiding frostbite. But the company snapped to attention when the captain appeared.

"At ease," Fraser said. As the men relaxed, he told them he wanted to talk about the war. Ben listened carefully. There was a lot going on that he did not understand.

"This war has created a political problem," the captain said in his crisp voice. "As you know, General MacArthur's job was to free North Korea. To do that, he said we had to bomb the enemy's supply bases in China. But the President is commander-in-

30

chief and he said no. That should have been the end of it, but MacArthur refused to back down. Truman fired him and gave the command to General Ridgway. Clearly, Truman felt that bombing China would start a bigger war in Asia. That would give the Soviets an excuse to march into western Europe."

"What does all this mean to us?" a soldier called out.

"It means we have to fight a limited war," Frasier said. "We're still trying to win, but we can't use our air power against China. Some people say it's like fighting with one hand tied. That may be so, but we have to live with it."

Late in May of 1951, the U.N. forces opened a big offensive. Ben hoped their firepower would overcome the Chinese edge in manpower. At first the drive went well. The U.N. armies pushed the enemy back all along the line. The 2nd Division fought its way from hill to hill in central Korea. After each battle there was always a new hill to take. **Casualties** were high on both sides. The communists dug in and built strong new defenses.

In mid-June, Captain Fraser spoke to

his men again. "Korea is much like World War I," he said. He was tired and some of the snap was gone from his voice. "We're fighting a war of position. Neither side can make a breakthrough. Each hill is a fortress. Only a direct hit from our big guns can take out the enemy's underground **bunkers**."

The mail from home brought more bad news. Mark showed Ben a clipping from a New York newspaper. "In Korea," the editorial read, "the enemy has five men for every three U.N. soldiers. Neither side can advance without suffering huge losses. In World War I, a million men died in the battle of Verdun. In much the same way, our casualties in Korea are growing. Is it time for the American people to demand an end to the war?"

"We can't give up now," Ben said. "If we do, our men will have died for nothing!" As he said that, Mark handed him another article. The writer pointed out that Chinese troops were giving up in large numbers. "Why," the article asked, "didn't the June offensive drive further into North Korea?"

"We were short of ammo and supplies!" Ben said angrily. "The roads were torn up. The monsoon rains flooded the rice paddies. Bad weather kept our planes from flying. Those writers should see Korea for themselves before they blame us!"

On June 23, 1951, the Soviet delegate to the U.N. proposed a **truce**. "The Soviets call the shots for all the communist countries," Ben told Mark. "The North Koreans and Chinese will listen to them. Maybe we will get a truce."

The peace talks started on July 8 at Kaesong [kay-song], a town on Korea's west coast. The talks bogged down almost at once. The two sides could not arrange a truce. Along the front lines, men were still dying.

The talks dragged on for weeks. Each side made demands that the other side would not accept. The U.N. delegates walked out to protest the presence of Chinese troops at the talks. When the delegates returned the communists put up a new roadblock. They refused to sign a truce until all foreign troops left Korea. The U.N. delegates turned them down. On August 23 the communists falsely accused U.N. troops of attacking Kaesong. The talks were broken off once more.

Months went by before the talks started again. In November the two sides met in a tent city at Panmunjom [pan-moon-jum]. All this time, the two armies were still shooting.

"Now they have a new problem," Ben groaned. "They can't agree on the return of prisoners of war. It's still fight-fight, talk-talk. And we're the ones who have to do the fighting!"

THE BATTLE OF HEARTBREAK RIDGE

"You keep up combat readiness by attacking!" General Van Fleet told his commanders.

To sharpen its fighting edge, 2nd Division was thrown against two strong enemy positions. The first target was a round valley known as the Punchbowl. Ben's regiment was ordered to take Hills 983, 940, and 773. The numbers referred to the height of each hill in meters.

The ridge line between the hills was honeycombed with North Korean tunnels. "South Korean troops couldn't take those hills," Captain Fraser said. "They had to withdraw after 12 days."

The men had read about the battle in the army newspaper Stars and Stripes. "The

ROK losses were brutal," Andy Dawes said. "It's no wonder they call it Bloody Ridge."

The 2nd Division's assault began with air strikes. On August 30 U.S. fighter planes dropped **napalm** on the ridge line. The jellied gasoline burned everything it touched. Then the planes flew **strafing** runs with machine gun and cannon fire.

As the planes flew off the regiment moved up the rocky hillside. Most of the North Koreans had waited out the air strikes in their underground bunkers. Now they popped up and hit back with machine guns and rifle grenades. Ben crept in close and lobbed a grenade into the gun slit of a bunker. Crossfire from a second bunker drove him back. The medical corpsmen who tended to the wounded were targets, too. Three of them went down.

The major in command of the regiment gave the order to pull back. Ben helped carry a wounded man down the hill. Near the bottom his combat boot caught between two rocks. His ankle twisted as he fell. Despite the pain, he hobbled back to a first aid station. A medic wrapped his sprained ankle. The men with more serious wounds were flown out in helicopters.

Despite the setback, Hill 773 fell that afternoon. With their position broken, the communists pulled out two days later. Bloody Ridge now belonged to the 2nd Division.

Mark found Ben in the field hospital. "Whoever named that place Bloody Ridge knew what he was talking about," Mark said. "Some guys in Company C were hit by our own artillery fire."

The battle for the ridges went on. Three miles north of Bloody Ridge lay another piece of high ground. It soon earned the name Heartbreak Ridge. The north-south ridge had three high points: Hills 894, 931, and 851. There were also some smaller hills, such as Hill 520.

For the troops, it was Bloody Ridge all over again. The North Koreans ducked into their tunnels to wait out the air strikes and artillery fire. Their **camouflaged** bunkers were hard to spot from a distance.

Ben's ankle healed quickly. He was back with his regiment for the September 14 attack on Heartbreak Ridge. The assault began at 5:30 that morning with a long artillery **barrage**. Despite the barrage, the North Koreans were ready. The communists rained mortar and artillery fire on the regiment as it moved forward. Once again, the regiment had to retreat.

Heartbreak Ridge was living up to its name. The division suffered 3,700 casualties in the first assaults. After that, the air force did its best to level the hills. Over the next month the flyboys hit the defenders with 250 tons of bombs. The army added 600,000 mortar and artillery shells.

On October 10 the infantry tried again. By now only Hills 851 and 520 remained in enemy hands. The order to take Hill 520 came down the chain of command. The message passed from 8th Army to X Corps to 2nd Division to 23rd Infantry Regiment. At the end of the line was Company G, 2nd Battalion. "That's us," Ben said. "Let's go get 'em!"

The bunkers on Hill 520 were only 200 yards from Company G's position. Artillery fire plastered the hill to keep the North Koreans under cover. The platoon moved out when the firing stopped. The men lugged a machine gun forward and set it up behind a small mound. The gun gave covering fire while a squad tried to **outflank** the first bunker.

All at once the GI machine gunner ran

out of ammo. Seeing their chance, some North Koreans rushed the position. Ben and his mates picked them off with their rifles. A brushfire broke out, hiding the bunkers in a curtain of smoke.

Ben led his platoon forward the last 60 yards. Mark was right behind him. The rocks made good cover. Ben turned and gave his friend a grim smile. "They're not going to beat us th—"

His words were cut off by a shell that exploded only 30 yards away. As the blast flattened him, Ben saw a GI blown into the air by the blast. **Shrapnel** thudded into his armored vest. He thanked his lucky stars that he was wearing it. To his left, someone opened up with a flamethrower.

The flamethrower did the trick. Eight North Koreans broke and ran from the last bunker. Twelve others surrendered. After three hours of hard fighting Company G had taken Hill 520.

A French unit took Hill 850 three days later. The Battle of Heartbreak Ridge was over.

AFTER THE BATTLE

Heartbreak Ridge was one more battle in a war that seemed to go on forever. At last, in July of 1953, the two sides agreed to a truce. The final stumbling block was the prisoners held by U.N. forces. Many of them did not want to go back to North Korea. The communists gave in and let each man make his own decision. A truce line was drawn near the line held by each army.

The long and bloody war taught both sides some lessons. The U.S. learned that leading the fight against communism could be costly. Over 30,000 Americans died to keep South Korea free. For their part, the communists learned that the free world would stand up to aggression. For North Korea and China the price of the lesson was written in more blood. The two countries lost over 600,000 men killed in action.

The truce did not end the arguments. Newspapers said that General Van Fleet should not have attacked Heartbreak Ridge. With the peace talks going on, why try to capture a few more hills? Van Fleet defended himself. He said that the attacks drove the enemy away from strong points that threatened his lines. Critics answered that the war was fought to save South Korea. It

Troop ship bringing soldiers home from Korea.

should not have been used as an excuse to hold live field exercises.

Ben Moore's tour of duty in Korea ended before the shooting stopped. At home his friends asked him if the war had been won or lost. He said, "It depends on your point of view. If the goal was to keep South

Korea free, we won. If you wanted to drive the communists out of Korea, we lost."

His answer pleased no one. Americans like to win wars. They do not like to see them end in a draw.

Ben's three-year enlistment ended in 1953. It was time to think about his future. On his uniform was the Silver Star he had won for bravery at Heartbreak Ridge. In the army that made him the equal of any man. Ben reenlisted and asked for duty in Germany. A second war in Asia sent him to Vietnam in 1963. Back in combat again, he was wounded in a communist ambush. The wound was his ticket home. He returned to Fort Ord in California, where he trained young soldiers.

Ben retired as a master sergeant in 1970. He is married now and owns a small garage. On weekends he coaches his son's Little League baseball team. Korea belongs to another lifetime.

GLOSSARY

Important Historic Figures

GENERAL DOUGLAS MacARTHUR (1880-1964)—Commanding general of the UN forces at the beginning of the Korean War.

GENERAL MATTHEW RIDGWAY (1895-)—American general who succeeded General MacArthur as commander of UN forces in Korea.

HARRY S. TRUMAN (1884-1972)—33rd President of the United States. Truman made the decision to send U.S. forces into Korea to resist Communist aggression.

GENERAL JAMES VAN FLEET (1892-)—Commanding general of the 8th Army in Korea. It was General Van Fleet who ordered the attacks on Bloody Ridge and Heartbreak Ridge.

44

Important Terms

BARRACKS—A building (or buildings) used to house soldiers.

BARRAGE—A heavy, sustained volume of artillery fire.

BUNKER—A fortified earthwork, often reinforced with timbers and sandbags.

CAMOUFLAGE—Any material that hides soldiers by making them blend into their natural surroundings.

CASUALTIES—Soldiers who are killed or wounded in action.

C-RATIONS—Canned foods that can be prepared quickly for troops in the field.

DEFERMENT—A legal postponement given to someone who is scheduled to be drafted into the army.

DRAFT—The forced selection of people for military service.

FOXHOLE—A shallow hole dug by a soldier as a way of avoiding enemy fire.

GI—A slang term for an American soldier. GI stands for "government issue," a term applied to anything provided by the army's supply department.

GOOKS—the GI's slang term for North Korean soldiers.

GRENADE—A small bomb meant to be thrown by hand or fired from a specially equipped rifle.

HUMAN SEA ATTACK—The tactic of sending masses of soldiers against enemy positions. The aim is to overwhelm the defenders no matter how great the attacker's own losses may be.

M-1 RIFLE—The standard infantry rifle during World War II and the Korean War. The .30-caliber M-1 held an 8-shot clip.

NAPALM—A jellied gasoline used in bombs and flamethrowers that burns everything it touches.

OUTFLANK—To attack an enemy position by hitting it from the side where it is weakest.

PLATOON—A basic fighting unit in the U.S. Army.

R&R—Army slang for Rest and Recuperation leave. R&R gives soldiers a chance to recover from the hardships of combat.

SHRAPNEL—Sharp fragments of metal produced by an exploding artillery shell.

STRAFING—To attack ground troops by firing on them from a low-flying plane.

TRUCE—An agreement to stop fighting while the two sides in a war try to work out a permanent peace treaty.

UNITED NATIONS (U.N.)—The organization formed after World War II to keep the peace. The U.N. does not have an army, but it can ask member nations to send troops to keep the peace.